Of Infinite Beauty
A Quaker explores Infinity

Robin W. Ahlgren

Publisher: Aporian Adventurers Press
Printer: Azimuth Print Ltd
February 2011

First published February 2011.

by

Aporian Adventurer Press

44 Saint Clement's Road,
Harrogate,
North Yorkshire,
United Kingdom

ISBN: 978-0-9568075-0-2

AMDG

CONTENTS

1 – *What is this book for?*

The purpose of this book is to delight the reader. It's meant to be fun! It doesn't have many conversations, but it is filled with beautiful pictures which are good to look at. If the reader just enjoys looking at the pictures, the book will have been worthwhile.

The book is called '*Of Infinite Beauty*' so surely, the reader will ask, there must be more to it than pretty pictures, a lot more? Yes. The book has two secret ingredients to go with the pictures.

There are some reflections on the meaning of life, and there's a teeny, tiny, little bit of mathematics.

Lots of people don't like maths. Don't worry. There are only one or two pages with maths on, *honest*. The maths won't get in the way. You can skip right over the mathematical bits. You can get a long way by ignoring mathematics. (Just look at the banking industry.)

That reminds me: there will also be a few jokes, but you don't have to take *them* seriously.

This is a book of infinite beauty and it has been written to be readable by anyone. If, like the author, you are one of the minority who *do* like maths, then you will have to look elsewhere for that. I'm sure you know where to get your fix.

It's OK if you want to ignore the hidden ingredients, I won't take offence. I'll be very happy if you just skim through my book looking for the most beautiful of the pictures.

It is a book by a Quaker, but it is not written only for Quakers. My main reason for writing the book is to show people a very famous and beautiful set of diagrams. I also want to explain why I find these diagrams interesting and meaningful. To me the diagrams are inspiring: they remind me of ideas that are important in my life.

These ideas are not new and, like all ideas, they are only important if they can be connected to real life. For the most part, mathematics is not about everyday life. It is just a game played by making meaningless marks on pieces of paper.

People find inspiration in poetry, painting, music, silence, or country walks. (To varying degrees, they all work for me.) My hope is that by sharing these pictures, and writing a few words about them, I can explain why I find them a source of inspiration. They might then become a source of inspiration for others too.

2 – Can we draw 'Infinity'?

For many years one of my more modest ambitions has been to write a book about infinity. Recently, while preparing for a meeting of Young Quakers, I discovered a fresh way of starting the book.

I had been wondering what the youngsters might enjoy on a Sunday morning. I came up with the idea that we might 'draw a picture of infinity'. I was a little apprehensive about trying such an abstract activity but, on the day, it worked out well. The children quickly got the hang of what we were trying to do. They tackled the job with enthusiasm and produced a large and impressive picture to display to the older Quakers.

In this section of the book I'll describe what the youngsters did.

We started with a large sheet of white paper with a big green square glued in the middle of it. It looked like this:

Area = 1 square metre

Perimeter = 4 metres

If the sides of this green square are each one metre long, the green area will be one square metre and the perimeter will be four metres. This is about the right size to fit on a table top with space for four children to sit round and work on it. (The real thing was just slightly smaller, but it's easier to explain if we stick to round figures.)

What I wanted to do was alter the square so that its boundary would be bigger. If we made it big enough, we would have a picture of infinity. The problem was that making the boundary bigger would make the area bigger, wouldn't it? We would run out of space on our piece of paper.

But what if we cut out a smaller square from the big green square and pasted it back on nearby?

This has interesting possibilities.

The area of green hasn't change, but the perimeter is a bit longer. The boundary along the top edge of the square is longer, as we can see from this next picture:

4

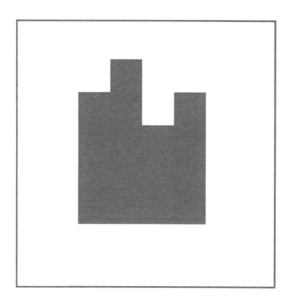

We all know what is going to happen next.

We could do the same thing on all four sides:

Area = 1 square metre
Perimeter = 8 metres

This is great fun for a small group of children sitting round a table and supplied with bits of green paper, bits of white paper, and some glue sticks.

5

I don't know what this shape is called. (It certainly isn't a square.) But I do know that its area is *still* one square metre. Whenever we cut a bit out of the square, we added it straight back on, so the area can't have changed. But the boundary *has* changed, because the length of every side has doubled. The not-a-square is now eight metres around.

The boundary of our green not-a-square has 28 sections. 24 of them are a quarter-metre long and there are four longer, half-metre sections.

We all know what is going to happen next.

We can do the cut and paste job again, for each section of the boundary of our new green shape.

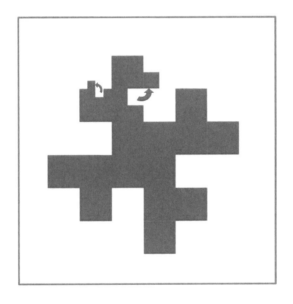

After we have done all 28 segments we will have this picture:

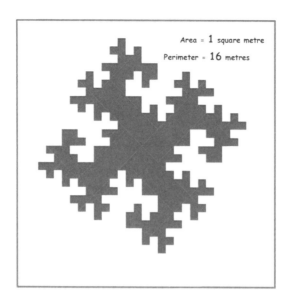

Area = 1 square metre
Perimeter = 16 metres

This is as far as the Young Quakers got. It is a lot of work to turn 28 edges into 196. As one of them said: "We tried to draw a picture of infinity, but we ran out of time!"

Knowing that some of my readers are on the look-out for ideas to entertain lively Quaker children, I must give some practical advice.

The project is easier if you start with a big sheet of white paper, the sort of flipchart sheet that is pre-printed with one inch squares.

Stick a big green square in the middle of your white sheet. Then, reduce the area of the green square by covering up the green you want to remove with squares of white paper. (This is much easier than trying to cut bits off a green square you have just stuck down.) Make some smaller green squares, to add on the extra bits and compensate for the bits you have covered up.

Once you have done all four sides of the square, the second stage can be done by using self-adhesive address labels: green ones for additions and white for subtractions.

We all know what is going to happen next.

We are going to add and subtract extra bits on each of the small sections of the new picture. They are only one sixteenth of a metre long, and there are 196 segments.

It would take a long time, but if you *did*, it would look like this:

Area = 1 square metre
Perimeter = 64 metres

We all know what is going to happen next.

We could, if there were world enough and time, cut-and-paste the segments of this new boundary (there are more than 1,000 of them, each just a few millimetres long) and get an even fuzzier picture: a nowhere-near-a-square.

If we kept on doing it, over and over again, we would end up with a picture of infinity. (If we had time.)

(This diagram looks very similar to the last one. The little ins and outs of the green are so small that the changes are too fine to be seen on a printed page.)

On a finite piece of paper we have drawn a picture of infinity.

As one of the Young Quakers said: "That's cooool!"

There is no greater happiness for a wrinkly old Quaker than to hear a young Quaker say their idea is "cooool".

3 – Is this what you call simple?

The green not-a-square reminds me of a Quaker Friend who asked me 'What is a fractal?' In reply I got out a notepad and sketched the process we've just seen. I started with a square, cut bits out, added bits on, and ended up with a very rough drawing of a fractal curve.

She followed what I was doing attentively and, when I was done, she asked 'Of what practical use is it?'

'None.' I said. 'It's completely useless. It's totally useless, like Michelangelo's sculptures or Mozart's symphonies.'

I told her about G.H. Hardy, an English mathematician from the early 1900's who often boasted: '*Nothing I have ever done is of the slightest practical use.*' He had also been known to propose as a toast: '*Here's to pure mathematics. May it never find an application.*' It has to be admitted that some mathematicians are interested in maths *in itself*, not as a means of achieving anything in the real world. After all, they don't spend a lot of time *there*.

"Anything that's finite is boring."

John H. Conway.
A pure mathematician.

But there *are* practical applications of fractals. For example, mobile phones need a long aerial to pick up a signal. *Fractal* aerials are ideal because they give great length in a small area.

Our green not-a-square is an example of a fractal. There are lots of fractals (an infinite number of them) and to say exactly what they are would mean using some maths, and I promised not to do that.

But their main characteristics can be described in plain English:

- They are *infinitely complex*. If you examine the fine details of a fractal you will find even finer details within it. The details go on and on forever.
- They are *self-similar*. Looking at the finer details of a fractal will reveal details that are similar in shape to the coarser details.
- They are constructed *recursively*. Each fractal is grown by repeated application of a *simple* rule.
- They are *natural*. Things in nature often have complex, self-similar structures, so mathematicians are interested in fractals as a way of understanding real objects.
- They are *fascinating* and *beautiful*.

Actually, they aren't *all* beautiful. The green not-a-square is not really beautiful. It may be interesting, especially if you actually try to draw it, but it is a rather fussy looking shape and not a great beauty. In fact, if I change the colour scheme I can make it look quite sinister.

There's a much prettier fractal known to mathematicians as Koch's Snowflake. Like the square it starts as a simple shape – a triangle – and by adding bits on (no bits get removed on this one) it too ends up with an infinite boundary around a finite area.

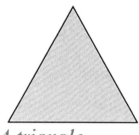

A triangle ...

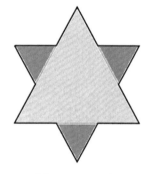

... add some points ...

... and keep going

Eventually, after a large number of additions, Koch's curve looks like this:

You can see why it is called 'the Snowflake'. (I have included a faint outline of the initial triangle, and the first round of additions, to show where this fractal came from.) It was invented in 1904 by a man from Stockholm called Helge von Koch.

Mathematicians get excited about these diagrams. They're interested to find very simple rules that give complex results

But there's a problem: the diagrams are hard to draw. Although the rules are simple, they have to be applied over and over again. It all gets very laborious.

But then along came computers. A computer is a tireless drudge and, unlike human beings, it copes well with the task of applying a simple rule over and over again. It doesn't get bored. It just keeps going. And so mathematicians found, in the 1960's, that they could use computers to explore lots of different kinds of fractal.

And now, after the Snowflake, we come to the star of our show.

Benoit Mandelbrot was born in Poland in 1924, brought up in France, and worked mainly in the United States of America. (Mathematics has always been a very international activity.) He invented the word '*fractal*' in 1975. He was the first man to explore one of the most famous and beautiful fractals, a shape called the Mandelbrot Set.

The simple rule for constructing our green not-a-square could be written as:

- Start with a square,
    - break every line into quarters,
    - cut a square out at each third quarter,
    - add it on at the second quarter, and then
- Do it again, and again, and again ...

Our green not-a-square began as a square.

Mandelbrot's set begins with a simple circle:

(Fractals don't *have* to be green.)

Next, we apply a simple rule.

The simple rule for Mandelbrot's Set is a simple equation.

Sorry about that folks.

It is a very simple equation.

(Simplicity is relative. *Pop goes the Weasel* is a simple tune, but I can't play it on the piano, nor on any other musical instrument.)

Brace yourselves. Here it is:

$$z_n = z_{n-1}^2 + z_0$$

I promise never to do that again!

But you don't have to understand this equation to see a picture of what it does.

If we apply the simple rule once, the equation makes the circle squashed and a little smaller. (The orange shape below.) Apply it again and it becomes smaller and a bit wobbly. (The green shape.)

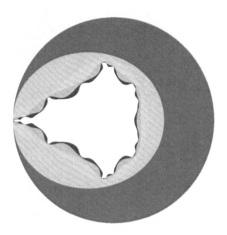

Another three applications of the rule give us the blue, purple and white shapes. Each shape fits inside the previous one and is a little more wobbly in its outline. Also, after the first two or three, each shape has a longer boundary than the last.

We all know what is going to happen next.

We're going to keep on doing this.

Yes, I know it isn't very beautiful yet, and it may be giving you a headache, but there is infinite beauty in store for you. I promise.

If it really does give you a headache, just skip this bit. I won't mind, and the book will still be beautiful. (That's the thing about infinity, if you take a bit of it away there is still a lot left.)

Here's what the rule does if you apply it 2,000 times:

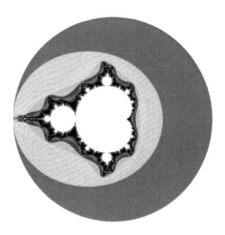

The white bit in the centre is now very complicated indeed. If you turn it on its side it looks a bit like a fat little Buddha:

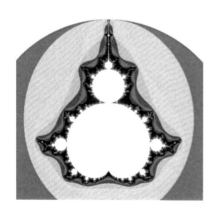

It still doesn't look very beautiful, but it is starting to look interesting. And if we look at its fine details in close up it looks more interesting still. Here's a picture of the whole thing:

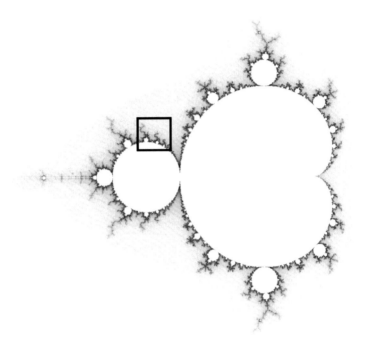

If I enlarge the details in the box we see this, much more lively picture:

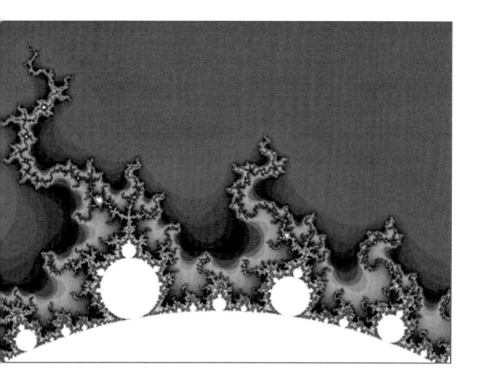

Now things are getting much more interesting.

Let's enlarge it a bit more:

This remarkable picture is just a small part of the original picture. It is a bit of the picture close to one of the circular buds attached to the big circle in the Buddha diagram – a chip on his shoulder perhaps. In the first diagram the details of this last diagram would fit inside one spot of ink from the big picture. It is a minute part of the whole viewed at a magnification of over 3,000 times.

This tiny detail has the remarkable property that it contains several copies of the white Buddha, the whole Mandelbrot Set. There's a biggish one about half way down on the right hand side, and many smaller ones dotted around the picture.

So, here's a picture that contains copies of itself. It's as though someone gave you a photograph of someone holding a photograph and, when you looked closely, the photograph they are holding in the picture is actually the original photograph itself.

Of course we all know that's impossible, so instead here's a picture of someone who *really* knows how to play *Pop Goes the Weasel*.

One of the remarkable things about the Mandelbrot Set is that it contains within it an infinite amount of detail. If we magnify any part of it we will find more details, and those details will have smaller details, and so on.

The degree of magnification can be as great as you like. Many of the pictures in this book are magnified so much that, to see them in the main picture, you would have to magnify it billions of billions of times.

"There are 100 billion stars in the galaxy. That used to be a huge number. But it's less than the deficit! We used to call them astronomical numbers. Now we should call them economical numbers.

Richard P. Feynman, Physicist

Here, just for fun, is a picture enlarged so many times that you would need to magnify this book's cover by a number with over 200 digits, and apply 'the rule' a million times, just to be able to see it.

22

It's hard to get a sense of how big that magnification is, but I'll give it a try.

Are you ready?

Here goes:

> *If the main picture was expanded until it filled the entire observable universe, stretching right out to the very farthest galaxies, this candy-striped picture would <u>still</u> be smaller than the nucleus of an atom.*

Pictures like this are just the start of the beauty to be found in the Mandelbrot Set. But I think the idea of magnifying things by billions and billions of times it is really 'cooool'.

Maybe we should now see a picture of the man we have to thank:

"Smooth shapes are very rare in the wild but extremely important in the ivory tower and the factory."

Benoit Mandelbrot
20-11-1924 to 14-10-2010.

4 – *What colour is Infinity?*

In what I've done so far, I haven't stuck to the same colours all the time. The diagrams are mathematical and, like geometry, they don't have any natural colour. So how do I choose the colours for these fractals?

One way of looking at the Mandelbrot Set would be to think of it as a contour map. As each step is taken we add another, higher contour to the map. Here are the first few contours again:

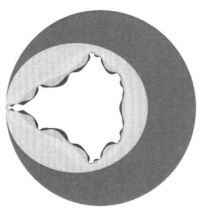 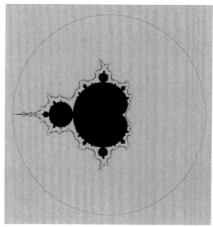

The map on the left shows the six contours, from each of the first six steps, filled in with contrasting colours. The map on the right has been simplified so that it shows only the first, eighth, ninth and thousandth contours as black lines on a green background.

If we add more contours, say the first twenty, to the green map we see more detail:

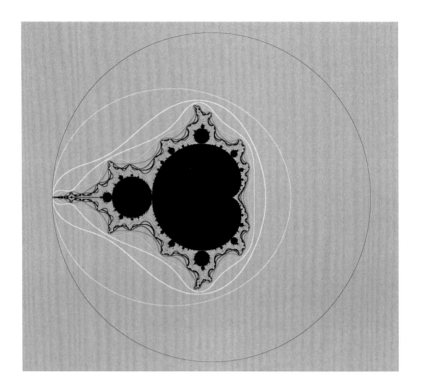

As we add more and more contours the equation we are using as our rule makes sure that every new contour is *inside* the last one, but *outside* the black, knobbly Buddha in the middle. At the same time, it makes sure that each successive contour is longer than the last. It doesn't take long for the contours to get very crowded.

The contours on a geographers map usually echo the colours of a normal landscape and the map makers often give us a guide looking something like this:

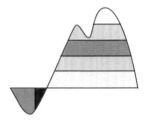

There's blue for the sea, and beige for the beaches, green for the lowlands, darker green for the hills, purple for the moors and white for the snowy mountain tops.

Putting the map maker's colour scheme on the Mandelbrot contours, we will get hills, mountains and valleys. We end up with a mathematical island looking like this:

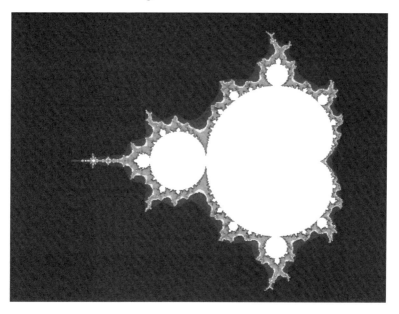

From a tourist's airplane seat, the island might look like this:

There, in a deep blue sea with a light blue sky behind, is an island with yellow sandy beaches, green forests, rocky highlands and a snow covered plateau to top it off.

Anyway, if you want to imagine the Mandelbrot Set as an island, choosing the right colour scheme for your contours will help. But it would be perfectly possible to pick a completely different colour code for the contours, perhaps something like this:

We could cover the mountain tops with a host of golden daffodils, adorn the slopes with red rhododendrons, blight the hills by shopping malls, pave the lowlands in tarmac and pollute the sea with oil. The shape of a map's contour lines may be fixed by geography, but the choice of colours is just a matter of taste.

The shape of the Mandelbrot diagrams is fixed by the mathematical properties of our simple equation. The colours are chosen by the computer user and are just a matter of taste. (Or lack of it.). This means that each diagram we produce can be coloured in a host of different ways. We can have a dramatic effect on the appearance of the diagram, and on our response to it, by carefully choosing the colour scheme. This means that there are three steps – three creative steps – in creating an image of a fractal:

- First we select *which fractal* we will use. We could have the green not-a-square or a prickly Koch snowflake or the Mandelbrot Set, or any of an infinite number of other fractals.
- Then we decide *which part* of the fractal we are going to look at in detail.
- Finally, we decide how to *colour* it in.

Now, prepare to be amazed.

Overleaf are four very different colourings of one set of contours. In each of these four pictures the contours are the same. But the colour schemes are very different.

They look like four totally different pictures:

28

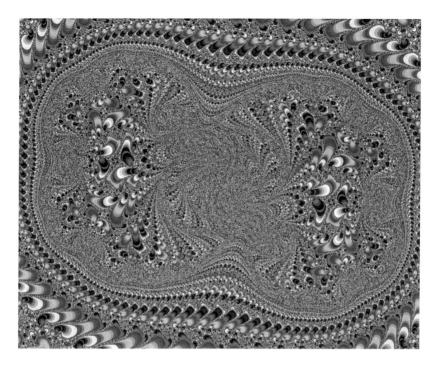

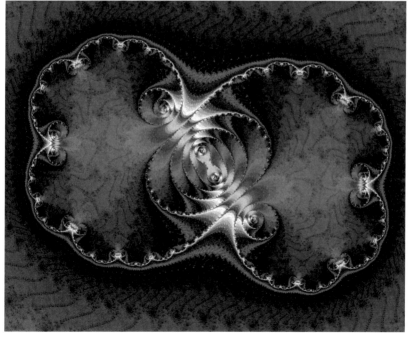

29

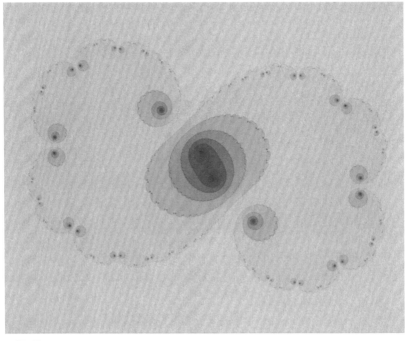

30

These four pictures show how different a single contour diagram can be with different colour schemes.

In the first of the four the contours change colour at every step of the process. (The picture is the result of applying our equation about 100,000 times and shows only a tiny part of the whole Set.) That's a bit like having contours on a mountain changing to a fresh colour for every extra millimetre above sea level. The result is a rather jumbled picture with some emphasis on the flatter parts, but no easily recognizeable shapes emerging.

The second picture – the one with a green corkscrew across its middle – has contours that change less often. Now we can see some interesting shapes: there are tiny little corkscrews around the picture, similar to the big one in the middle, and big purple searchlights illuminating two bays which are full of convoluted tapestries and chains.

The third picture makes the contours broader still. Now the emphasis shifts to spirals: a large central spiral around a small dumbbell shape, two medium spirals to left and right of it, and a flock of smaller spirals (in pairs) around the bays. The network of chains is still there, but the searchlights are less obvious.

Finally, the fourth picture has very broad contours. Now the tangled chains in the two bays have disappeared and the scene is dominated by broad green spirals against a turquoise background.

But it doesn't end here. Within the big Mandelbrot diagram there is a huge variety of shapes and pictures to be found – a whole menagerie!

On the next few pages are just a few examples. All of these shapes are embedded somewhere or other in the diagram. You just have to find the right bit, magnify the picture by the right amount, apply the simple equation a few hundred thousand times, and *hey presto!* we have another picture.

Here's a selection. See how you like them.

Demonic
whirlwinds...

Fighting
Dragons ...

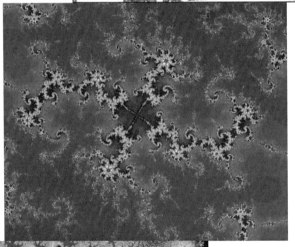

Antique
embroidery ...

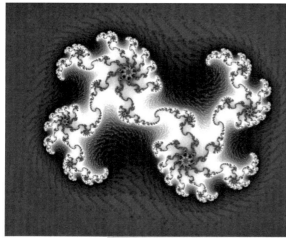

Celtic
tracery ...

Alien
brain-scan,

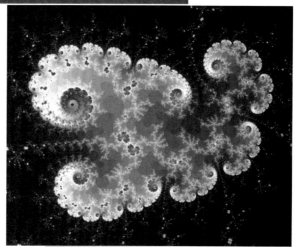

Peacock
Processions,

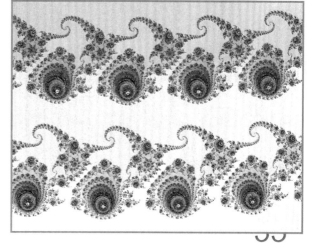

Or even a psychotic octopus, like this:

It is amazing and bewildering, but the original Buddha shape really does contain all these other shapes within it.

"There is no abstract art. You must always start with something. Afterward you can remove all traces of reality."

Pablo Picasso

Whatever Picasso meant when he said '*you must always start with something*' it seems that the Mandelbrot gives us a whole lot of abstract designs by starting with just one equation. (Does an equation count as 'a thing'? Also, you need a printer. And a very powerful computer. But nowadays they give those away for free with telephone contracts.)

What we need now is some way of finding our way around in these infinite diagrams.

35

5 – Can you see the Pattern?

The Mandelbrot Set is so big and complicated that it can seem overwhelming. However, the layout is far from random. Unlike real islands and lakes, there are lots of systematic patterns we can use to find our way around.

In the next few pages I'm going to take a tour of the Set, following the direction of the arrows on the diagram.

The first set of patterns can be found by looking at the 'buds' around the 'heart'. The heart is the largest white area on the diagram below. If we were posh, and I'm not, we could call it a cardioid. But that's just a swanky way of saying 'heart-shape'.

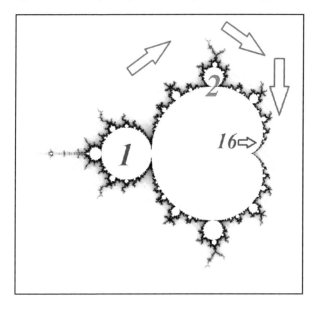

There are small circular knobs – I call them buds – all around the heart. They vary a lot in size from the biggest (on the left hand side of the heart and about a quarter of its size) down to buds too small to be visible. I've marked the first bud '1', the second (at the top of the heart) as '2', and I've marked where the sixteenth island is, though it's too small to see on this diagram.

(In writing about this, or speaking about it, it doesn't really help that all the buds have mini-buds adhering to them. I will try to be consistent: a bud is a circle attached to the heart. A mini-bud is a small circle attached to a circle. And mini-buds have micro-buds attached to them ... Oh, dear! It just goes on and on.)

And as imagination bodies forth
The forms of things unknown, the poet's pen
Turns them to shapes, and gives to airy nothing
A local habitation and a name.

Shakespeare
A Midsummer Night's Dream, V(i)

As we go round the heart we will find the buds change in a systematic way.

The first bud is really just a circle with a long thin spike on it.

The second bud is a circle with spiky twigs sticking out.

The third bud has more twigs.

As we go round three things happen.

- The buds get steadily smaller. They all look the same size in these pictures, because I have magnified them to be the same size. I have marked the amount of magnification relative to the first bud on each picture. The second bud is magnified three times: x3, the third by six times: x6, round to the sixteenth, magnified x375.
- The twigs attached to each successive bud become more and more complicated. The first bud has one straight twig, the second has twigs that branch into two, the twigs on the third branch into threes, the sixteenth into 16.
- As the islands get smaller, the twigs become smoother, more rounded, more like ferns and less like sticks.

"The mathematician's patterns, like the painter's or the poet's must be beautiful; the ideas, like the colours or the words must fit together in a harmonious way. Beauty is the first test: there is no permanent place in this world for ugly mathematics."

G.H. Hardy (1940)

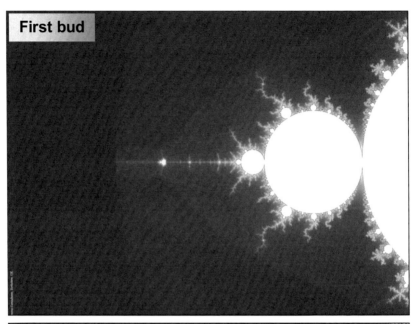

First bud

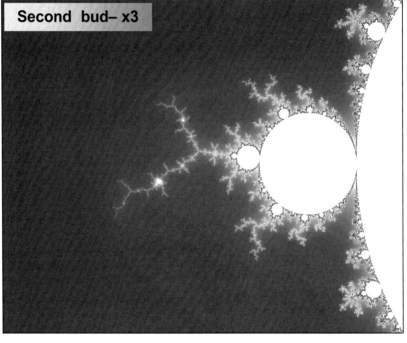

Second bud– x3

40

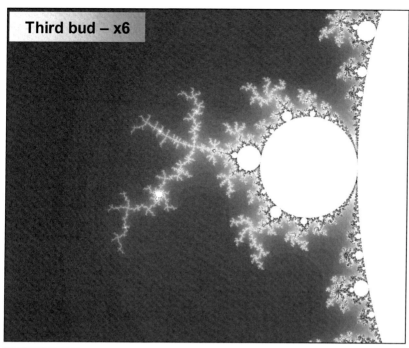

Third bud – x6

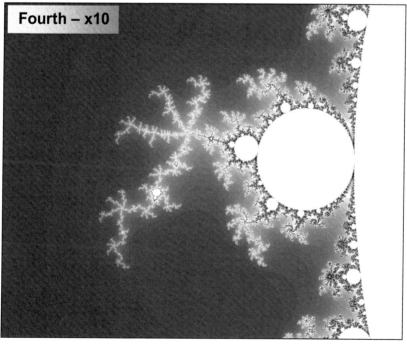

Fourth – x10

41

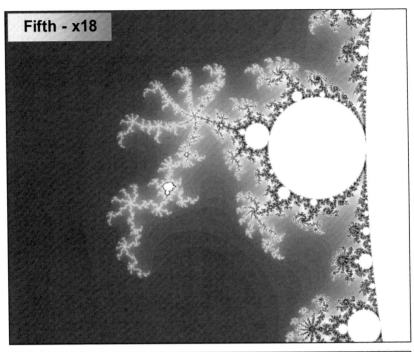

Fifth - x18

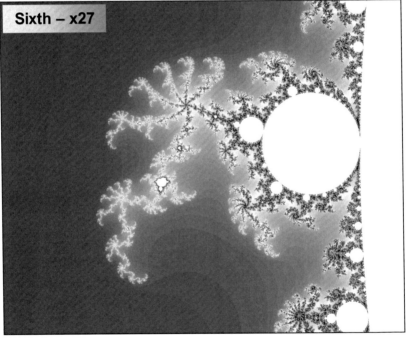

Sixth – x27

42

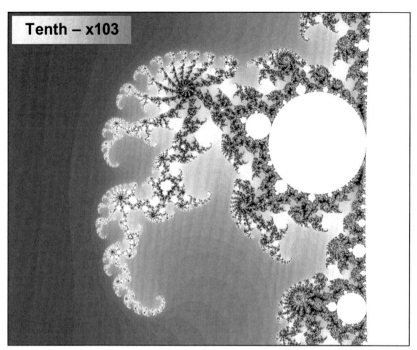

Tenth – x103

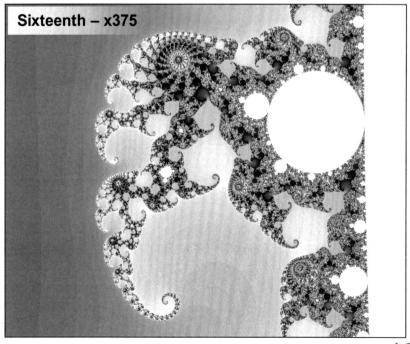

Sixteenth – x375

43

I suppose what I *should* have said is that *four* things happen as you go round:

- Buds get smaller.
- Twigs proliferate.
- Sticks become ferns.
- *Each picture is more beautiful than the last.*

That last one, the sixteenth, looks like an elephant in a sunset. It's one of those Indian elephants, with an ornate headdress.

But that's not the only regularity in the Mandelbrot Set.

You will have spotted that next to each bud, on the main twig, there is a little copy of the Mandelbrot Set. I call these *islands*. The big island has little islands upon his back to bite him, the little islands have lesser islands, and so ad infinitum.

Footnote for pedants: *Strictly speaking, "the Mandelbrot Set" is the area (usually white) in the centre of my main picture. It's just the heart, plus the bud, plus the little replica sets. The beautiful curves and swirls, lie just outside the set itself.*

Phutt-phutt note for academics: *Strictly speaking, these aren't footnotes because they're not at the foot of the page.*

Do I look bovvered?

The next few pages highlight the biggest island from each of the bud pictures. Once again, I have made a note of how much magnification is needed, compared to the picture of Bud-1, to see these islands.

To see the first island clearly we have to magnify the picture 16 times. The sixteenth island requires a magnification of more than 2,000.

Here's the island sequence:

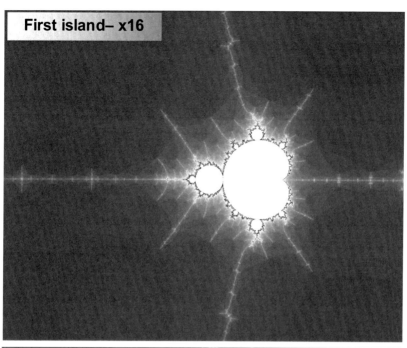

First island– x16

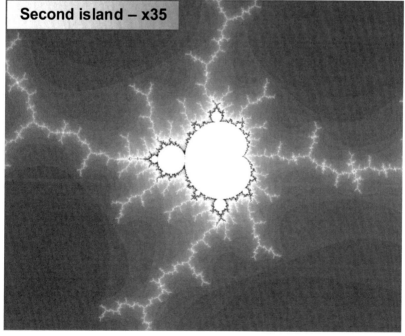

Second island – x35

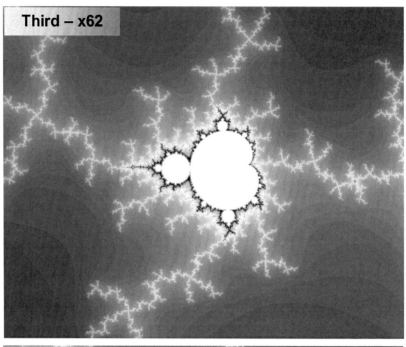

Third – x62

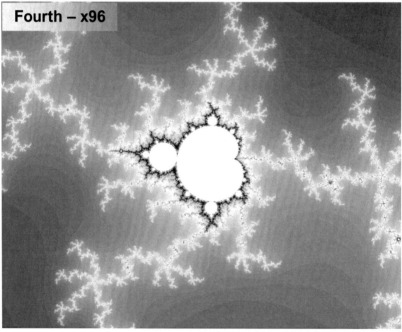

Fourth – x96

46

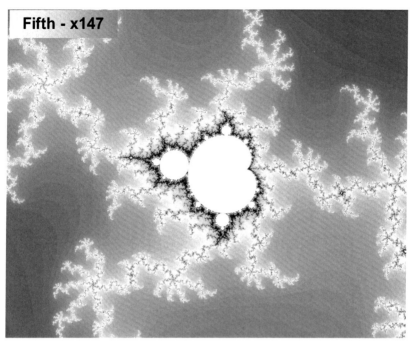

Fifth - x147

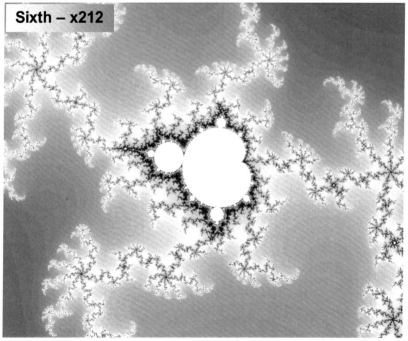

Sixth – x212

47

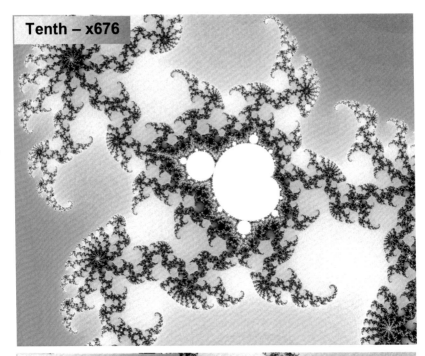

Tenth – x676

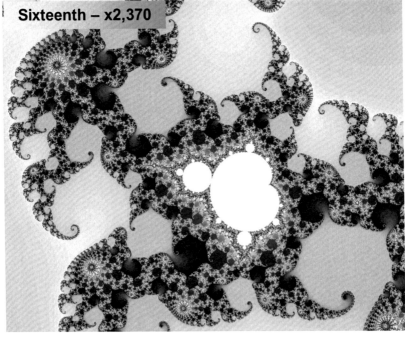

Sixteenth – x2,370

48

Once again, there is a consistent pattern.

- Each island is smaller than the last. However, the islands get smaller at a slower rate than the buds. The first island is sixteen times as small as its bud. The sixteenth island is only seven times smaller than the sixteenth bud. (Later islands get down to about six times smaller, but no more.)
- Each island's twigs share the same degree of *bushiness* with their buds. Bud number five has twig with branch points where it breaks into five and island number five is surrounded by a forest of five-branched trees. Island number ten has a ten branched forest, and so on.
- The distortion on the islands becomes more marked as we go round. The lower lobe of each heart is much bigger than the top lobe and the spike (the bit pointing to the left) becomes more twisted.
- In general the patterns become more curved and *ferny* as we go along.
- And, *of course*, everything becomes more and more beautiful. Just think what island 200 would look like! (Sorry, but it is so small and detailed that it would take too long for my computer to draw it.)

The big feature of all these patterns is that as we look at smaller and smaller islands we find there is more and more detail. The complexity grows, and it has to be packed into smaller and smaller amounts of space.

The patterns don't stop there.

Every bud has twigs, but there's more than one island on each twig. If we select one bud – let's say the tenth – we can search along the main twig and seek mini-islands.

There are plenty to find. In fact there are an infinite number of islands on any twig. I would like to prove that to you, but I haven't the time, and anyway, it would make the book too big.

Here's a selection of islands from the tenth twig:

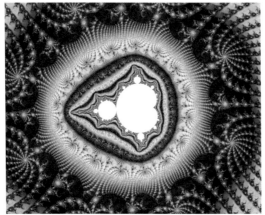

These islands all lie on the main twig of the tenth bud.

This first one is very close to the tenth bud.

It is almost perfectly symmetrical.

This next island is found by moving a little further outwards along the tenth twig, a bit further away from the main bud.

These two islands have a dense array of twigs around them, but there are still ten branches at each break point.

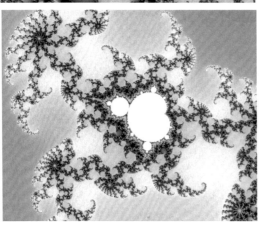

This is the biggest island on the main twig of the tenth bud. (This picture has already been shown in the sequence of islands.)

It is the least symmetrical island on the tenth twig.

his is a small island on the
ɪain twig of the tenth bud. It is
ıst a little further out than the
ɪiggest island, further along the
vig and further away from the
ɪg heart shape.

t a glance, it looks similar to
ɪe biggest island, but it is
ɪfferent. It has more symmetry,
ɪd the bushiness is smaller,
ɪlative to the island itself.

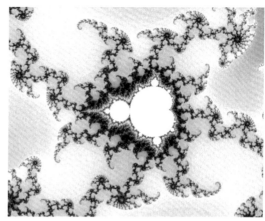

ɪis island is an even smaller
ɪand on the main twig of the
ɪth bud. It is even further out
ɪm the biggest island.

ɪlooks quite different to the
ɪggest island. It is completely
ɪmmetrical and the bushiness
ɪw consists of long chains of
ɪgs.

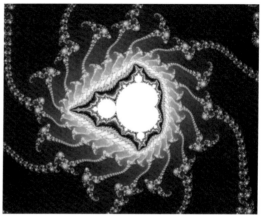

(Magnification: 10 million.)

ɪally, this is a *minute* island.
ɪs almost at the tip of the
ɪth bud's main twig and a
ɪg way from the big heart
ɪpe.

ɪ bushiness now looks like
ɪy long, fine chains combed
ɪ neat spirals.

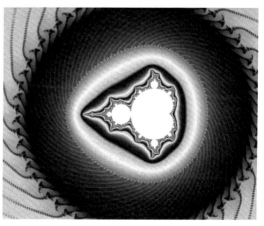

(Magnification: 5 thousand, million,
ɪlion, million, million, million times.)

51

You may think that the neighbourhood of this last island is filled with thin, red and blue lines. But those fine lines are actually packed with detail. Here's an enlargement of part of the inner turquoise band from the last picture. (It's over two-thirds of a million, million, million, million, million, million times enlarged compared with the first bud.) (There were six millions in there.)

Here we see a dozen links from two of the long chains in the island's outer regions. If you look closely you can see that each link is made up of the 'elephant's head' shapes from the tenth bud. Also, every link has the same property of 'ten-ness' that the tenth bud has.

52

Not only that, but if we magnified it even more, we would find lots more copies of the island inside every link of the chain, and every copy would be surrounded by fine chains with hundreds of links each containing ...

(It quickly becomes boring to keep read phrases like '*over two-thirds of a million, million, million, million, million, million.*' It's like listening to a politician talking about his achievements. Or a fisherman. And I don't think it really helps anyone to grasp how big or small things are. It doesn't help me, anyway. Once you've made your first million, it's just more of the same. So, for the most part, I will stop saying how big each picture is. They are *all* highly magnified. Get the picture?)

These patterns, the regularities in the Mandelbrot Set, make it possible to see where each picture came from. Every picture is a kind of fingerprint. You can work out which bud it is attached to by counting the number of branches from each twig. You can work out how far from the main heart shape it is buy counting the number of links in each chain, the number of twists in each spiral, and so on.

Although the patterns are infinite and complex, the patterns are so strong that it is possible to find your way around. It's as if every part of the Set is, in itself, a little notice board saying '*You Are Here*'.

And yet, because there are so many complications, it is very difficult to find your place *in practice*. When I find a really pretty picture I need to note exactly *where* I found it. With such an abundance of similar pictures I will never find *that one* again. It would be like seeing a very pretty daisy in a huge meadow. If you went back to the same meadow later in the day you would be very lucky to find *exactly the same daisy* a second time.

54

6 – How many patterns are there?

After that introduction to buds and islands, I'm going to give up the *systematic* exploration of the Mandelbrot Set. (I just haven't got the heart for it.)

However, serendipitous exploration is very enjoyable. The software I use (a program called *Fractal Extreme*) allows me to look at pictures and enlarge bits that look interesting. It also allows me to alter the colour schemes, rotate pictures, make movies that zoom in and out of the detail and remember the locations of pictures. It's a clever piece of writing.

The process of searching for 'interesting bits' can be very absorbing. Though I have spent lots of time exploring the Set, I still find myself saying 'Wow, that's a surprise.' I have got the hang of how Mandelbrot Isle is organised and yet, it is so complex that I am still finding new things to look at. The first time I came across a psychotic octopus (see page 33) I was so surprised and delighted that I laughed out loud.

Do not get me wrong, I am no Train Spotting Anorak. My passion is for the fascinating variations in the detailed track layouts at Signal Cabins.

Quote from a train spotting blog.

For the finer details (the greater magnifications) you do have to be patient. Some of the diagrams in this book have taken several hours of computer time to produce. But I have come across an

55

extraordinary range of images and I would like to present some of them now.

Sometimes images remind me of other things, things in the real world, and I have added some of these reminders into my gallery.

For example, I have dubbed one favourite set of patterns 'Chains'. It's easy to see why. (I think.) Here we can see four chains of earwigs wrapped into a spiral.

Other details remind me of owls.

This is an Eagle Owl.

Many of the diagrams look quite biological:

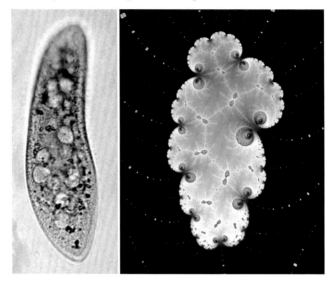

Some are very delicate, like Japanese embroidery:

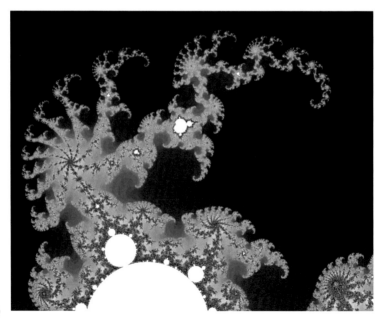

There are short chains, with only a few links, and weird dancers.

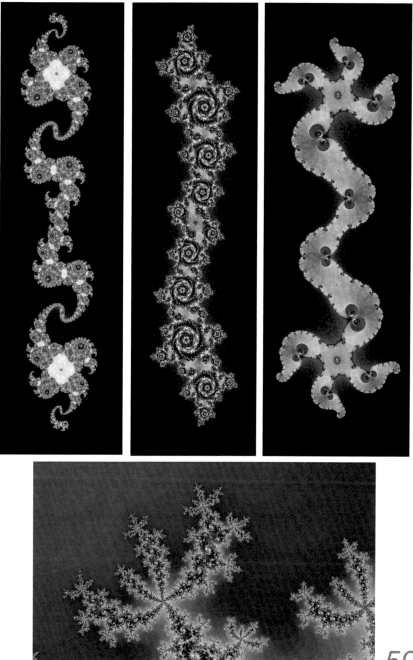

This is not an Eagle Owl.

There are rotors and rosettes:

This catalogue is endless, almost infinite.

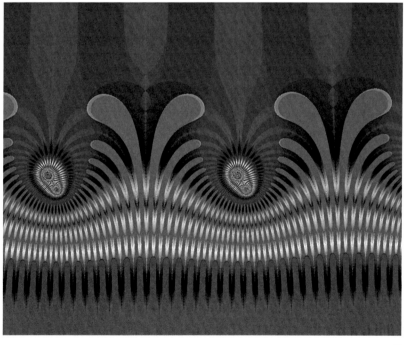

Even lowly worm finds his place.

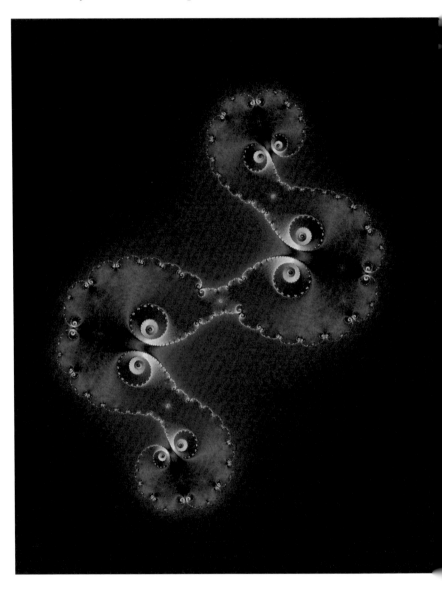

And there's one that reminds me of a map of Japan.

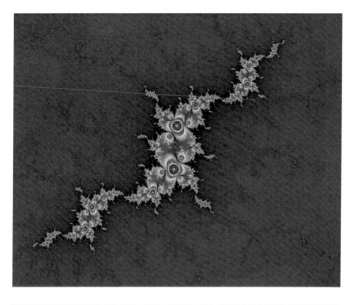

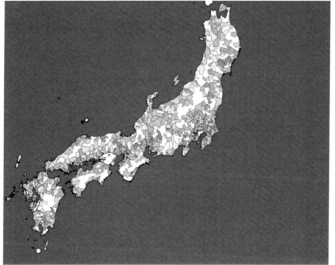

This what you see if you bowl over a mushroom.

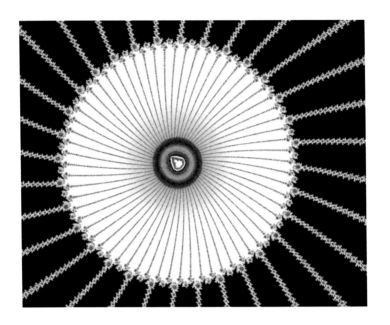

Ferns are a good example of a fractal plant. They have a stem with leaves branching off it. The leaves are in the same form: a mini-stem with leaflets branching off that, and so on.

Part of the variety in these pictures is a result of my efforts to choose colour schemes which accentuate different aspects of each picture, or to give some variation just to please the eye. But most of the variation comes from the Mandelbrot Set itself.

The original green not-a-square doesn't contain the same variety. Enlarged versions of the not-a-square will just look like the original. It is still a remarkable shape. It has a huge boundary even though it covers only a small area. Even though the young Quakers only had time to do the first two stages of the process, they ended with a shape that had almost as big a perimeter as the large hall they were working in.

Most fractals are closer to the green not-a-square , and to Koch's Snowflake, than they are to the Mandelbrot Set. Many of them just look fuzzy – like clouds – or leafy like ferns.

The Mandelbrot Set is unusual because it has an infinite variety of beautiful details within it.

7 – Could things be simpler?

There is one final property of Mandelbrot's fractal I want to mention – its *connectedness*. It isn't always obvious, but every bit of the Mandelbrot Set is connected to the main cardioids.

In the picture below, which shows Bud-3, we can see the usual big island, upper right, and several small islands. The main twig of Bid-3 splits into three twigs at a crossroads.

On each arm of the crossroads there is a small island, much smaller than the big island, but still visible as a white dot against the black core of the twig. You can also see some little islands in the black twigs emerging from the mini-buds around the main bud.

There are lots more islands (Yes, an infinite number of them.) on all the twigs in the picture, but most are too small to be seen.

What *can* be seen is the black lines running along the twigs. These are a sort of filament connecting every single island to its own bud. The filament is actually white, it is part of the main Mandelbrot Set, but it is such a fine filament that you can't see it on this scale. It is buried in the middle of every black twig in the picture.

This becomes more obvious if I show you a very fine detail shot from the long straight spike to the right of Bud-1.

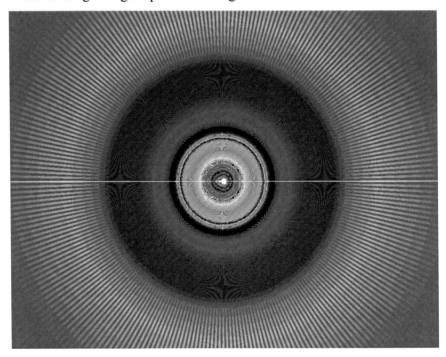

This is magnified a huge number of times – a 1 followed by 465 zeroes. It is also very close to the end of the long spike. So near that if we magnified the main picture to be the size of the observable

70

universe, this tiny island would be less and an electron's width from the end of the spike. Running across the whole picture there is a single, thin, straight white line. This is the filament that connects every bit of the long spike to Bud-1.

It is more difficult to see the filament on other pictures because it is so thin. But it is there.

Every island, not just the ones on the straight spike, but every island in the whole Set, is connected by a filament to the bud, and through that to the heart shape.

These gossamer threads remind me of two things. First, they remind me of this quote:

No man is an island entire of itself; every man is a piece of the continent, a part of the main;

John Donne

We may try to be autonomous – and we live in an age when individuality is stressed – but we are actually connected to all the other people we meet, and to all the people we never meet.

Not only that, but Quakers are connected to other groups. Some among us may like to think of Quakers as more grown-up than other, more traditional, Christian churches but we need to remember our links. And we are also connected to Buddhists, Hindus, scientific atheists, humanists and even mathematicians.

The Mandelbrot Set reminds me to think of the human family as linked and related. Some of our links may be indirect, and to people with a very different outlook to our own, but we are all linked. The Set includes islands with spikes, islands set in calm, ferny bays, and islands set in sparse, jagged landscapes. All are connected.

You may object and say that I have magicked a religious rabbit out of a mathematical hat. But I am not saying I have *proved* that there are connections, I am just using the set as a metaphor – a mathematical parable, if you like.

The second thing the filaments remind me of is that the universe is often fractal by nature, and it is all heavily interconnected. My own, now very rusty, expertise is in astrophysics.

We see the fractal nature of the universe at very large scales. The picture below is a map of the galaxies around our own.

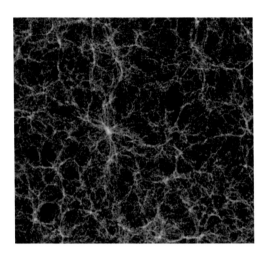

In this picture every tiny dot is a galaxy, or a cluster of galaxies. The picture shows that the galaxies are not scattered randomly or uniformly. They gather in large structures containing hundreds of thousands of galaxies.

We even find similar structures, but for different reasons, in smaller objects like this supernova remnant. The remains of an exploded star spread out in threads and bubbles which look like the tangles of some of our Mandelbrot pictures. (Though the Mandelbrot is more regular and organised.)

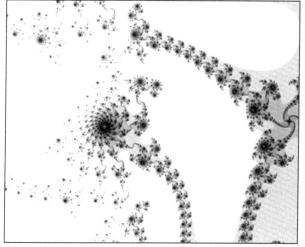

I'm not suggesting that these pictures are 'all the same sort of thing'. They certainly aren't. But science has discovered that there are deep links between the behaviour of very big things (clusters of galaxies) and very small things (protons, neutrons and electrons). The theories physicists develop are linked by strong filaments – not of physical material, but of interconnected ideas.

Because the theories are all connected we are begining to see that the old compartments of science are not watertight.

73

*If you want to make an apple
pie from scratch, you must
first create the universe.*

Carl Sagan

It's not just physics, either.

Biologists know that the evolution of animals depends on whole communities of competing and co-operating species. And, inside the animals, a rich network of microscopic structures and chemical processes makes their behaviour impossible to understand in simple terms or in isolation from other animals.

Everything is connected, and our understanding must complement the old scientific skill of analysis – breaking things into their component parts – with a new skill of synthesis.

Who knows, even economists might join in?

*The sage sees all the universe
without leaving his cell.*

(Traditional.)

8 – Is Infinity real?

The classical Greeks used to debate whether 1 could be a number. Their problem was that numbers need to be *plural*, surely. But we all know that 1 is 1, and all alone, and ever more shall be so.

Archimedes will be remembered when Aeschylus is forgotten, because languages die and mathematical ideas do not. "Immortality" may be a silly word, but probably a mathematician has the best chance of whatever it may mean.

GH Hardy

The Greeks were also unhappy about infinity. They didn't like to say that there is an infinite number of numbers. They preferred to say that the number of numbers was *potentially* infinite. Actual infinity they were not sure about.

True, between faces almost any number
Might come in handy, and One is always real;
But which could any face call good, for calling
Infinity a number does not make it one.

WH Auden

This uncertainty continues to the present day. One modern mathematician felt that the theory of infinite sets is a mistake, a dream we will eventually wake from and see that it was just a nightmare.

And physicists sometimes ask if there is actually anything physical which can be infinite. After all, if every little electron is connected to an infinite number of influences, how can it ever make up its mind what it is going to do. (Yes, I know that's a childish way to put it, but there is a real debate about the number and range of effects we need to deal with.)

And what about my infinite not-a-square? Suppose we drew a really detailed version of the green not-a-square and put one corner of it under a microscope. What would we see?

Well, we are talking about a *physical* drawing here. So it would be made of atoms. If we etched our not-a-square into a crystal of salt, and looked at it through a very fine microscope, we would see something like this:

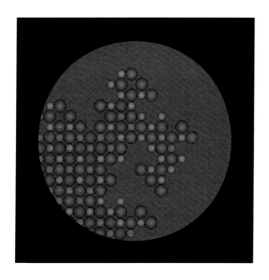

(The sodium atoms are blue and the chlorine atoms are brownish orange. Actually, they are *ions*, but you get the picture, don't you.)

The point is that, *in the real world*, infinity is never possible. We eventually come up against the graininess of the world, the bits and pieces the world is made of. I suppose you could try to split the atom, but the very word *atom* means *indivisible*. (Those Greeks again!) Eventually we come up against physical barriers to our infinite ideas.

We may try to draw infinity, but we never actually *see* it.

I am incapable of conceiving infinity,
and yet I do not accept finity.

Simone de Beauvoir
(or is it Princess Anne?)

In the physical world as it is, we may never get to infinity. And yet we need it. Mathematicians, for all their disquiet, have found infinity a vital tool for their work. They have even invented many different infinities, all of them big and some of them infinitely bigger than others. Some of these infinities are even described, *by their inventors*, as 'indescribable'.

Physicists, even though they are always dealing with finite objects, use mathematical methods which assume that infinity exists.

We can't manage without it.

And maybe, even if it isn't there in the real world, it is there in our minds. I can *think* about infinity, so it exists – if only as a thought.

Imagination is more important than knowledge. Knowledge is limited. Imagination is infinite.

Albert Einstein

And I think we need infinity in our lives. We need that sense of direction which only the infinite can bring. We may call it God, or 'the Light', or Allah, or Awareness. But whatever we call it, we can't live well without it.

Acknowledgements

- I am grateful to my wife (who can play much more than just *Pop Goes the Weasel*) for her encouragement, editorial skills and patience.
- The Mandelbrot pictures were produced using Fractal eXtreme, a program sold by Cygnus Software. (They have a website at www.cygnus-software.com which also provides a simplified version for free).
- The perspective picture of Mandelbrot Island was produced using Fractint, a free computer program available on the Internet.
- I would also like to thank the Young Quakers of Harrogate. They inspired me to dig this dusty project out of my files and bring it back to life and to completion in a finite time.
- Smudge, the cat, appears by kind permission of her carers, Hilary and Stephen Prosser. (I have been unable to contact the carers of the Eagle Owl.)
- Most of the non-Mandelbrot photographs have been taken from the *Wikipedia Commons* website. The remainder were taken by myself.
- I drew all the diagrams myself, using OpenOffice software.
- The book was printed by Azimuth Print Ltd., Bristol, U.K. who have a website at www.azimuthprint.co.uk

Robin W. Ahlgren.
Harrogate, U.K.
February 2011